There's no Present Like ......Time

GW00775716

by

Pauline Birchall

MAPLE
PUBLISHERS

There's no Present Like ......Time

Author: Pauline Birchall

Copyright © Pauline Birchall (2024)

The right of Pauline Birchall to be identified as author of this work has been asserted by the author in accordance with section 77 and 78 of the Copyright, Designs and Patents Act 1988.

First Published in 2024

ISBN 978-1-915796-87-5 (Paperback)
    978-1-83538-030-7 (E-Book)

Book Cover and Layout by:
    White Magic Studios
    www.whitemagicstudios.co.uk

Published by:
    Maple Publishers
    Fairbourne Drive, Atterbury,
    Milton Keynes,
    MK10 9RG, UK
    www.maplepublishers.com

A CIP catalogue record for this title is available from the British Library.

PREFACE

I started writing these quirky poems and tales shortly after 6th July 2015

My partner of 3 years, at that time, had just undergone a successful maxillectomy to remove a tumour from his upper jaw. The after treatment required several doses of radiation followed by an arduous routine of learning to eat and swallow again.

We had always lived in our own separate houses, so I would sit in my bed most evenings armed with my iPad, find a photograph from the numerous pictures of our adventures together, highlight the memory on my screen, then set about writing a witty or humorous connection to that particular scene and of course all dedicated to the man himself. The idea behind this labour of love was to provide a constant means of support for the days and months ahead, allowing Indie a smile, plus the knowledge he was totally loved and admired during what was to become eighteen months of endless trauma. I would email each picture and verse for him to savour. He absolutely loved and devoured every one, with always a reply of mirth and gratitude for the same. As I now had a huge collection of these picture/writings, I found a local print company near to my place of work and between the owner Robbie and I, we produced three separate books, which I gave to Indie for his birthday, our anniversary of meeting and Christmas during 2016 as a momento of legacy and admiration for my brave warrior.

Although the initial operation was successful, sadly the cancer returned twice over the following year. Indie battled ferociously throughout. In his own words "This bugger is not going to beat me" In early 2018 he became part of a new immunotherapy trial at The Royal Marsden Hospital in London. The treatment appeared to shrink the final tumour, which had manifested itself in an inoperable position at the back of his throat. There was now renewed hope for future. Tragically the heavy duty medication and radical treatment had taken its toll on his body. On the 26th July 2018 at 7.30pm, Indie passed away peacefully in his sleep, at home, whilst resting in his favourite chair. Surrounded by precious artefacts of many worldwide travels that were a monument to his love of adventure. What more fitting a place to gently close his weary eyes and drift toward the finality of life on earth, moving beyond, to whatever lies ahead for us all. Never an ending... Just the place where you leave the story.

I am now combining all three books into one complete storytelling scenario. So very proud of these writings, in the face of adversity, I thought It would be endearing to share these poems and stories with a global audience.

I really hope my book brings the warmth of a smile to anyone who reads it.

All of the content comes from the heart... a tribute to the most amazing person who lived and loved life to the max. I was so fortunate and blessed to have met Paul back in 2012. My lover, storyteller and mentor took me on this awakening journey of adventure, for which I will be forever grateful. To have had that one chance in a lifetime of new horizons and self-discovery, aided and abetted, is something I shall cherish till my end of days.

DEDICATION

Take This Book From The Heart <3

Savor All The Words Spoken & Unspoken On Our Many Walks

Hold My Profound Optimism Should The Story Unfold In Dark Corners

Chapter By Chapter It Chronicles The Tale Of Two Individuals

Blessed By The Joys Of Living, Caring & Sharing In The Moment

The Pages Offer Up A Cascade Of Bright, Shiny Adventures

Each Paragraph Conjures Up A Story Unique To Ourselves

A Tale Not Without The Travesty Of Injustice Or Dire Circumstance

Yet.. As In All Good Novels The Hero And Heroine

<3 Survive All Adversity To Live Another Day Of Future Passed <3

OUR FIRST DATE…. SATURDAY 7PM, HOVE, 17TH NOVEMBER 2012

The frission of jangling in the pit of my stomach is playing havoc with preparation for my first encounter with Indie Dancer. Our meet to greet phone conversation, a week ago, gave me much cause for curiosity, due to fact he had said " cuban heels, combined with a fedora would be part of his attire and on my arrival at Hove station car park, I was to look out for a dark blue car with rope securing a large ladder to the roof rack. For some strange reason of imagination I have this vision of a ponytailed ageing, hippy traveller, emerging from a battered, brightly decorated sixties VW camper van. As Indie comes across in conversation as extremely intelligent and eloquent of verse, complimented by a deep husky tone of voice, none of his descriptive of arrival makes any sense. I am perplexed.

Indie is taking me for a Thai meal in Hove at a tried and tested authentic restaurant. I love Thai cuisine so this part of the date will be delightful. Then on to Ralli Hall, a short walk away, to introduce me to his world of salsa and bachata dance. I hold much trepidation of this second half of the evening, as coordination is not my strong point. Think of the phrase two left feet! Well I possess two right ones as I am left-handed. Opposites attract mayhem. Arms that make the funky chicken look like Kentucky fried in flight, complete the overall look of flailing disco on the dance floor. I learnt to waltz, as a child, by standing on my dad's two feet, allowing him to orchestrate the one, two, three movements. Trying the same method with Indie may not cut it in the world of Salsa dancing.

Having dressed in my favorite little black Lipsy number, with an opaque silver and bronze patterned not too mini skirt bottom, to give an overall look of sassy yet classy. Beige patent Dune court shoes with five inch heels, give me great height (Indie is six foot two to my five foot five) Finally the whole outfit is adorned with matching black, shiny onyx necklace, silver bracelet and hoop earrings, I take one last look in the mirror and smile at myself with approval. "You look shit hot mature lady, just pray this isn't a case of beauty and the beast"

On this very dark November night, with the faint whiff of woodsmoke in the chilly evening air. I have arrived at my destination of assignation feeling very curious, almost fearful of what I am about to encounter. Looking amongst the sparse cars spread around Hove station car park I glimpse no vehicles remotely laddered or metallic blue in bodywork. Guessing my early arrival is maybe not such a great idea, I park up near to the metal railings separating the platform area from the car park. There are plenty of spaces either side of my car for him to park, assuming he hasn't got cold feet and decided on a no show.

The train station lighting around me is voluminous so hopefully Indie will spot my BMW immediately. Now I am getting fidgety, the butterfly cramps are building gradually. A few minutes pass by far too slowly, then I see his car, although I still cannot focus on himself as the windows are too dark, almost tinted. Relief ensues, as the car is a modern, executive style, shiny metallic royal blue , with no apparent dints or rusty bits and the ladder, although a bit of an eyesore, is neatly roped onto proper roof bars, giving the impression of an off duty posh window cleaner. Beside my car, to the right, he parks and out he steps. I take one last sharp intake of breath and my mouth drops open just a little as I step out of my car and am confronted by this handsome tall man, dressed in very flattering tapered black, trendy trousers and yes the promised cuban heels and fedora hat are in place but he is wearing what I can only describe as an anorak, come possible ski jacket in two tone grey, with red piping to the bodice and sleeves. This does not quite mesh with the overall Indie Dancer look. His flowing grey locks are tied into a pony tail poking out at the back of his jaunty black leather fedora with plaited trim and a feather tucked into it's side. It's a bit like Spanish Dancer meets Trainspotter. I am now faintly amused and trying very hard to supress my smirk, as I give him a genteel hug of greeting. " Hi Mr Indie J. You certainly live up to your promised descriptive of man and motor. Love the hat and the boots are just so cool, they flatter your long legs. I am impressed." Before I can cheekily ask what has happened to the long leather coat to complete the what should be overall look of Lee Van Cleef, he immediately apologizes for the grey anorak, with the most amazing smile of cheekiness that melts my heart, giving it cause to flutter. His eyes reflect sparkle of the same mirth. " I feel the cold very easily Polly, this is my thermal armor but I assure you there are no long johns lurking underneath" I give him a hug of forgiveness for the fashion faux pas and off we head to Thai Connection, as we are both in agreement that hunger and eagerness to enjoy good food is now paramount.

Portland Road is bustling with Saturday night diners and revelers heading in all directions to their various destinations, as Indie strides alongside of me, with a click clacking sound of cuban heels hitting slippery uneven paving stones. He seems so tall and distinguished, the glow of the street lamps seem to highlight his tanned complexion. Our conversation is giddy, interspersed with trial and error exercise of holding hands that is comfortable for us both. His compliments regarding my dress sense and statement of " You are absolutely stunning Polly, with the most beautiful smile, which certainly lives up to your oodle description on the dating site" , are extremely well received with a quiet satisfaction of 'Actually you genuinely mean all of that without any agenda or falsehood'. This adoration is to become one of Indie J's most endearing traits for me, as we embark on a journey of immense discovery. I already feel a sense of excitement and daring in the company of this extremely interesting man. My butterflies soar to a crescendo of anticipation, yet caution slips in as I have led a very safe existence thus far.

What a beautiful, authentic restaurant he has chosen. Warm bright colors of reds and oranges tinged with gold leaf compliment the ornately carved dark wooden tables and maroon velvet upholstered chairs. Dragons and lanterns are hanging down almost floating in mid air. Cooking scents of lemongrass and coconut tickle my taste buds. The Thai meal chosen with relish certainly lives up to great expectation. Conversation flows like a runaway train and three times throughout the meal, this lovely man produces gifts of delight, well thought out from various topics we had talked about in previous phone calls. My first package is an ornate notepad decorated with delicate purple and lemon butterflies, complimented by silvery bejeweled wings, handed to me during our starter of butterfly prawns and spring rolls. Very apt and ingratiating. I feel really bad, as giving gifts are definitely not my norm on a first date. Generally just getting through decent dialogue and searching for mutual chemistry is a gift in itself for most would be matches. The second gift Indie produces, in a crumpled waitrose carrier bag, causes me to be somewhat taken aback after the first beautifully wrapped offering. I peek inside, Indie has already enthused about his love of nature, backed up by the true fact that he walks every day if possible, at least five miles of serious trekking at a fast pace.

Earlier today he had completed a four mile circuit around Wakehurst Place, near Ardingly, admiring, as well as photographing some of the many autumnal colours of various trees and foliage displaying their vibrancy of seasonal beauty throughout the grounds. Inside this battered bag is an assortment of leaves depicting variety and colour of some great English trees in all their natural finery. I lay them gently on the white linen tablecloth, trying very hard not to crush any of them. Indie looks very pleased with his choices as I gasp with delight at the content and thought process of this very special offering. One of the pretty Thai waitresses serving our food is very taken with this array of nature lying beside my plate, so I look for a nod of approval from the giver before inviting her to choose a couple of leaves to take for herself. She is so genuinely delighted and I am really happy and gracious enough to share part of my keepsake with her.

My third and final gift, by now I am completely overwhelmed by this mans generosity, is a token of what comes next on the agenda later this evening. As I unwrap the CD of Bachata music, my heart sinks. Not because the gift is disliked or unwanted but it is a sore reminder of my trepidation as to how on earth I am going to cope with learning Latin american dance with a man who by his own admission, has danced his way over the past twenty years, in pretty impressive style, throughout most of the Latino countries, taking as partners some of the most stunning female dancers on the planet. 'Hells Bells' I am on a hiding to nothing here.

The date up to this point is just absolutely perfect. This much travelled adventurer is funny, sexy, handsome, so very interesting to listen to. A natural born storyteller, whose exploration and passion for the many countries visited, complimented by his real enthusiasm for native people and cultures encountered along the way, is an aphrodisiac potent enough to imbue me with a lust for 'More Please Sir'. I am totally entranced by the nature of the beast. Continuance is definitely a must have as we pick up our coats, being the gentleman of course he helps me on with mine, and head off into the freezing cold, dark autumn night toward 'Dances With Dragons'

The pavement is quite slippery with a layer of autumnal evening dampness. Woodsmoke fills the air with it's wonderful clawing aroma, as we walk back to Indie's car to retrieve his dance shoes. This could prove awkward as I never gave my footwear a second thought other than height and killer heels to impress. Hanging onto his arm for support, I feel heady of the pungeont night air, plus too many glasses of the very expensive malbec red wine he so graciously ordered and paid for, along with the rest of the bill for the delicious Thai food we so enjoyed. Arguing my corner for halves on a first date, I lose admirably to his gentlemanly gesture of "The warmth of your company tonight Polly is a delight to be rewarded with my treat for you, please accept this gesture from the heart" I cave in, but on the strict understanding that should he be still up for a second date after the dance session, my purse will be emptied in reciprocation of his generosity. He relunctantly agrees.

We have now reached the laddered motor car, parked at the station. My Pollyanna curiosity gets the better of me. I ask the question. "Why do you have a very long ladder roped to the roof of your car?" I had been too shell shocked to ask that question at the time of our meet and greet phone conversation. "Well Polly, you tell me. Do you remember some of our initial conversation when we first spoke on the phone?, plus the clue is in the profiling." He winked, raising his right eyebrow very sexily. Now I have to admit that just occasionally 'slow on the uptake' creeps in. This is definitely one of those moments. " I know you are not a window cleaner so that rules out the obvious. Is it a failsafe piece of equipment because you lock yourself out of the house often? " He laughs out loud at my barmy northern humour. " Think about it my pretty one," he grins, " if it's not for climbing up then what is the next feasible use? Think about my extreme hobbies" Aargh I really need to think on my feet now. " Got it " I yell in triumph. " It's to do with your Hangliding" " Yes oh clever butterfly you've got it at last" The dumb blonde card is now very definitely about to come into play "Do you put the ladder up the side of a hill, wherever you are, so you can climb up easily with the hanglider? " I ask with conviction. Now Indie is absolutely howling with laughter in his gruff, sexy manner. His gorgeous blue eyes sparkle with amusement. "You are so cute in your naivety my funny princess, I shall look forward to educating you Pygmalion style. The ladder is permanently secured to the roof of the car to hold my hanglider firmly in place when travelling, as the slightest dent in the framework would be a total catastrophe in flight." "Oh yes of course, it all makes sense now. Simple when you know why and how." I chuckle.

My heart skips several beats as my mind plays havoc with the Pygmalion comment. I allow myself an inner smile. 'This could be a very interesting journey of educating Polly in the art of endless possibilities'. Slipping my arm back through his, a shiver runs down my spine. Is this the result of the chilly night climate or a foreboding of hidden depths lurking within my new found Indie explorer, striding confidently alongside me in his black, highly polished Cuban heels. All of this concern is now brushed aside as I my ears pick up the strain of a very vibrant Latin American rhythm coming from behind the tall sash windows of the grey stone building in front of us just across the road. We have arrived at Ralli Hall to the heady sound of a live band. My nerves are jangling with anticipation and excitement of my first foray into his extreme world of salsa and bachata dance. He is going to need the patience of a saint for sure teaching me Latin American footwork.

The interior of the building is ancient, careworn but historically ornate, with very high ceilings and an impressive polished mahogany staircase situated just behind the tall, beautifully carved oak wooden double doors we have now come through. I am hanging on very tight to Indie's hand, the whites of my knuckles are visible as he leads me through a massive throng of writhing and wiggling dancers to the makeshift bar in the far corner of the dance hall. " What would you like to drink Polly? They serve a pretty mean mojita if you would like some dutch courage before your foray into salsa." I kick him on the shin playfully as I take stock of the very sexy, rythmic-dancing being skillfully played out on the highly polished wooden dance floor. The music is so exciting and intoxicating I find myself swaying and toe tapping to the one two three beat. My mojita is very alcoholic, the white rum burns at my throat, whilst the fresh mint soothes my palette for contrast of taste. " Are you ready to salsa", he grins at me with the most disarming smile, sparkling in it's own unique sexiness. My glass safely deposited on the nearest table, I follow him to a darkened corner of the room where he takes me into a very close embrace then twirls me expertly around several times. I am beginning to feel a sensual stirring within that allows me pure excitement, yet scares me somehow and I am not sure if that is nerves of failure to learn the moves, or the strange effect this man dressed all in black with the ponytailed silver grey hair is having on my psyche. " Just follow me with the basic one two three steps, practice makes perfect, you will be very safe, I promise not to make anything difficult for you. I am a very good teacher and my pleasure will be watching you smile with enjoyment as you become more confident with your ability to salsa." " How long have you got then? " I chide cheekily. " All the time in the world " he graciously replies.

The night progresses with practice and patience allowing me to feel a little more confident with the steps in time to the rhythm of frenetic salsa music being constantly played by a very honed and enthusiastic Colombian DJ called Danny O who, dressed in combats and extremely tight black vest T shirt, looks as though he has just stepped off the set of Good Morning Vietnam. Indie gives us both a break, whilst asking in the most polite, gentlemanly manner " Would you mind Polly if I ask one of 'the wigglies' to dance. I won't if it will bother you seeing me performing my accomplishments with another female ." " No you go ahead Indie Dancer, I shall enjoy watching you as I am sure I have well and truly cramped your style so far this evening." He approaches a stunning looking Latin American girl who looks young enough to be his grandaughter. I later learn her name is Louisa and she is normally with her Bachata teaching boyfriend Javier. Dressed in skintight black jeans and a beautiful lilac chiffon floaty top with threads of silver edged around the low cut neckline, she glides across the floor in her strappy, silver high heeled sandals. Both her and my Indie mentor hold each other very close as the sensual strains of a bachata dance begin, allowing a heady atmosphere to take over the room. I watch in awe and amazement. Never have I seen a dance so sexy and erotic in it's orchestration of music and bodies as this one. I am in awe of this mans expertise, yet so gutted that it's not me out there blending into his every move like a panther gliding for prey. "Bachata teachers across the land always use the catchphrase to the guys in the class, Love De Girl", he conveys to me as he guides me back to the dance floor for another round of sensual tuition, now of the bachata variety. I am eager and so very hungry to experience the nature of this dance.

Despite my protestations he insists on spending the remainder of the evening practicing and honing my salsa and bachata steps as best he can. I have to admit that after many forward and backward body movements, crazy twists and twirls, my body is actually falling back into the timing with the one two three rhythm of the salsa, when I falter or overbalance. Now I am starting to feel quite tired, it's 1am Sunday morning, yet pure adrenalin of excitement in this man's company is allowing me to stay standing. We wander hand in hand to the bachata room, where we have already visited twice to allow me to experience the closeness and sensuality of this beautiful, intimate dance. Indie grabs his Fedora on route from the coat rack, placing it on his head he tips it at a very jaunty angle, masking part of his face.

The room is surprisingly empty, seductively lit with subdued pale pink and blue spot lights, in all four corners of the ceiling, giving off a soft purple hue of atmospheric colour. I sit on a conveniently placed chair for respite. The music is intoxicating, headiness of all is beginning to overwhelm me and then it happens. This amazing guy, with the ponytailed hair, dressed sexily in black attire with Argentinian fedora, commences to dance bachata before me solo. Hypnotized by the scintillating, rhythmic moves he now orchestrates, sensual mood of music and highly erotic atmosphere, I am completely and utterly lost in the moment, so turned on by the total eroticism of this beautiful dance, the likes of which I have never experienced in a lifetime. This tantalising, enthralling showcase of mastered bodily movement is now ending and in one final gesture of sexual allure, Indie lifts up his elegant left hand, holds the brim of the tilted fedora with his slender long fingers and tips it downward and toward me with a look that holds every possible fantasy I could ever imagine or wish for.

Coats redeemed and smiles on both of our faces, we step out into the early morning foggy air. It's now 2.30am and I don't want to go home. We are greeted by a very beautiful, hazy full moon shining above us in a dark, indigo sky. Indie stops me in my tracks and tilts my chin upward. "Polly look at the beautiful harvest moon, millions of miles away, yet close enough to admire. Smiling down upon two people lucky enough to have walked within it's luminous glow tonight.. Very special, just like you." Caught in the moment I hug this crazy man and reply, "We are creatures of the universe, trashed in adversity yet thrown together by fate." My heart swells with anticipation of a journey yet to be encountered, stretching out a path before me full of learning and pure excitement.

Pandora Now Wishes To Open Up This Box

The Book is

A FITTING TRIBUTE TO MY INTREPID INDIE J x

MY INDIE J x

THE MAN WHO BROUGHT HIS OWN STORYTELLING

INTO MY WORLD AND ENRICHED MY DAYS WITH CONTENT OF THE SAME >!<!<

The Many Sides of My Intrepid Indie J x. World traveller drawn to wildernesses: Whether exploring the jungles of Borneo, climbing volcanoes in Ecuador, crossing the Sahara on camels or diving off the Great Barrier Reef, Indie loves new worlds & making friends across cultures. -Naturalist/conservation researcher: Indie tracks black rhinos & studies rare pangolin's in the Namibian bush. Avid hang glider pilot who has flown in California, Australia, Brazil & S. Africa. He drops everything to step into the sky when the wind is right! -Circus trapeze & aerialist student. He is stronger and fitter now than ever! -Passionate salsa & Bachata dancer. If you cut Indie, he bleeds Latin music. In Cuba & all over South America he frequently wows locals with his dancing. -Falconer: Another love in Indie's life is Luna, a beautiful great horned owl. -Sculptor in wood & stone. Indie studied Shona carving in Zimbabwe. -Poet with a quirky sense of humour. He relishes story-telling & theatre. - Oxford physicist: A Research Fellow for Philips, Indie developed 40 patents, taught at Stanford University & worked with the MIT Media Lab on social networking long before Facebook. -Social entrepreneur & Winston Churchill Fellow: Indie worked with local communities to help bridge the 'digital divide' in poor Brazilian shantytowns. The Tuareg in Mali made Indie an honorary brother for his work in Timbuktu. Sensitive, gentle man of honour & integrity Indie has more passion for life than anyone I have ever known.

TRANSITION

DAY 1... Monday 6th July 2015

A walk of finality had taken place on Saturday morning. Such closeness, hands gently intertwined, striding out along the top of Ditchling beacon. The warm gentle wind blowing away the cobwebs of despair. Very few words were spoken, there was no need of conversation about what was to come, just our own private thoughts of anguish around this whole crazy situation.

One final kiss through the open window of your car as you drove away, intact for a while longer. That kiss has to be remembered for a lifetime because life has dealt you the cruelest of battering. The big C has reared its ugly head and manifested itself over a six week period from a simple mouth ulcer on your gum, to full blown mouth cancer resulting in the Maxillectomy you will undergo at some point today at The Queen Victoria Hospital in East Grinstead.

Defiant as ever, your final pre op evening was spent at Richmond, doing what you excel at. Salsa and Bachata dance is one of your many facets and honed of the talent you have perfected over the years. Sunday evening would have seen you intoxicated and lost in the music and flirtatious nature of it's Latin American origins. I have sent you a late text as I just crave just one final goodnight speak before the dread of dawn to Transition.

"Hi Indie J x hope you lost yourself in the dancing tonight xx text me when you get home and I'll quick call before you go to bed. I read Will's post op blog. V clear on what to expect. I am scared for you. Nothing in his blog phased me. Geared up to support you in anyway I can. I have a game plan to get back up north tomorrow. Xx >!< xX

1a.m. ... So desperate to speak with you. It is the early hours, but you choose to stay silent and I have to respect your choices of privacy. I send you one last text of support, it's the only channel I have left open to me at this time of the morning.

"Am guessing you need to be left alone tonight   I would probably do the same if it were me. I wish I could just hold you to try to give you comfort and ease your turmoil. >!< Goodnight my brave Warrior Dragon. dream of Owls and Butterflies sitting on each shoulder, giving you the strength to sustain you over the next few days >!< xxxxxx"

I shouldn't even be here, in my own bed right now, as I had left yesterday to drive to Rochdale on a pre booked trip to take my dear ol dad to Wales for a weeks holiday. I had said my goodbyes to you, early yesterday morning, in a lighthearted almost jovial conversation, which had disguised our individual worries of what was to come. For whatever reason, I made it as far as Pease Pottage Services, where I had safely driven after a red oil light came on in the car, motor power was lost and braking seemed non existent. The AA operative attending was baffled as to the fault and had advised me to return home and get the car checked out today. To risk such a long journey ahead was suicidal, even for Ms. Gung Ho Polly !!!

6am. ...Sleep has been sporadic. I keep trying to put myself into your head, so I can try to read your thoughts and ease your mind somehow. I go through the different scenarios of playing out the next few hours of hospital waiting and preparation. You will be in deep, dark anguish. The constant of beating myself up for not being there with you has overtaken me. It was never going to be allowed, even had I not been scheduled to be up north, you would have chosen to go on this arduous journey alone, so I have to respect that decision, but it doesn't make my anguish and solitude, at this moment, any easier to bear. I send you one final text at 6am

">!< >!< >!< BUTTERFLY KISSES ON GENTLE GOSSAMER WINGS >!< >!<

8am. ...At last the ping goes on my mobile and I pray it's a message from you. There are two.

"Hi Ms P. In hosp theatre reception in gown! Dancing was good last night. Sorry we didn't get time 2 talk but thinking of u & yr love & caring & our joy..TBC xx gd luck getting up N to Pa today, hire car or garage fix"

"How u getting up north today? Mu + TAU, yr defiant warrior xxx" My heart races with excitement of contact, half naked, I click away my reply to you with humour spilt out from sheer relief.

"Bet you look pretty weird in NHS GARB x Its looking like hire car as Rob snowed under at garage. Just waiting on my car hire contact to call me as to what's available, as I need an automatic for self safety x What time is your op? How ru? I've started writing OUR TRANSITION BLOG at 6am today. It will keep me focused I HOPE.. MU BADLY X >!<"

8.30am. I decide I really need to hear your voice and I know you will be pleased to listen to my Polly Tones, so I grab the phone and ring your mobile. Verbal falling over words and catch up conversation is now the essence of time, as you will shortly be heading into that room of highly skilled people who will make some changes cosmetically, but will allow you longevity and a chance to resume your full on crazy lifestyle. I trill you my usual northern Tarrar, Tarrar at the end of our very smiley few minutes of togetherness speak, enveloped with the spirit of mega tight hugs time and tide deny us both at this moment. My private tears and anger flow freely now, whilst making the bed, at the sheer injustice of all of this but I am helpless to change anything. I feel sick and nervous to my stomach. Uneasy of outcome, yet my sixth sense reassures me all will be fine. This flipping song of George Michael's once again plays loudly in my head, over and over as it has, now constant, for this past week. Same part verse of lyrics every time.

"Here in the dark in these final hours, I will lay down my heart to feel the power but you won't, cause I can't make you love me if you don't"

A daunting song indeed and one of my favorites but I am beginning to find it dark and bothersome. Maybe once this is all over it will fade away. I send you a final text of encouragement, betwixt my tears.

"Keep the owl and the butterfly in sight pretty please xx TAU with great love and admiration for your bravery My Indie Dragon xx >!< xx"

2.30pm. ...I am awaiting the replacement hire car at The Marina in Brighton, so I can resume my trip to Pa's and Wales. The car is late of delivery, so I sit in the glorious sunshine at the cafe bar next door, soaking up the searing rays and thinking "If you are aware right now of this beautiful sunny day, you would be gutted not to be a part of it on one of your daily walks of life. "My mobile pings and I scrabble frantically to read the message. A trillion butterflies are circling my insides as I read your text with fear of dread. I should have known it would all be safe and ok of outcome.

"Woozy, coming round in Ross Tilley ward. Swallowing difficult with big plate, so choc milk shake but no pain yet"

4pm. ...I am finally on the road North out of Brighton, amongst the painful pre rush hour traffic clogging up the roads. I have to now weave through all of this mayhem, as my decision has been firmly made to bestow on my Indie J x a surprise "Pit Stop" at The Queen Victoria Hospital, East Grinstead. The need is overwhelming for a hug with my man. Yet again, I am now stuck in a long line of cars towards Woodingdean when my mobile pings. "Sod the motors behind, I am not crawling any further forward until I have read your text of progress. "I grab my glasses and hold up the queue.

"Hi B'fly. I'me not woozy now. Jus sore and v difficult to swallow & gaga dribbly !!!! Xx Whats happening for u?"

5pm. ...An hour of cursing the British motorists and their queuing bad habits, a few wrong routes and a helpful taxi controller with a good head for pointing me in the right direction, sees me hurtle through the gates of your current resting place. The Queen Victoria Hospital looks aged and worn like an old cardigan but boy oh boy do they but do some amazing work here with cranial surgery and their world famous Macindoe Burns Unit. I know you feel fuzzy, yet already bucking the system, according to your text. My need of urgency to see this for myself prompts me to rush down the odour tainted corridors like a bat out of hell, searching for the

Ross Tilly Ward, which is your current residence. A very helpful nurse points me to your bay and I really don't know what to expect as I stride to bed 3. Tubes, drips, monitors, maybe groans of discomfort?? Guess what?? My warrior is nowhere to be seen and the bed is empty. Then I hear those deep, dulcet tones unique in their volume. I follow the gruff and I suddenly see that oh so familiar face, talking and gesticulating animately to possibly your surgeon in a lovely, leafy quadrant garden outside the ward. Your Indie grunge attire is so relevant. Combat jeans, overlaid with non complimentary hospital gown accessory, hair tied back in signature pony tail and open canvas sandals.

Once the medic man departs, I sneak into the quadrant garden, creeping up behind you with the quiet stealth of a panther. You are perched on a plastic chair in the sunshine, with head down almost to the floor. My heart reaches out in comfort, as I assume throes of despair have overtaken your traumatic situation. I place my hands, from behind you, gently over those smiley eyes that never cease to create provocative responses. "Who on earth is that? "you chuckle.

"Cool hands on my shoulders" you chide. "The flittery, fluttery one "Is my response. Up you jump in amazement, with the biggest smile possible, under the current circumstance. Your eyes shine like a planetarium of reflective stars. Massive hugs of excitement in abundance. Then... what does this crazy man do?? Whips off the hospital gown and proceeds to twirl me round and round, Bachata style, in this garden of colourful place, with the hot sun drenching us both in all it's glory. What a truly magical, in the moment, crazy gesture. I am captivated and enamoured by my Indie Maverick already fighting his corner.

Turns out the head in hands of despair is actually Indie sending out bulletins via his mobile, placed on the ground between his feet to protect it from the sun. "Despair indeed.. Oh ye of little faith "

I leave this place, after one more ginormous hug of "squeeze me tighter please," with a lighthearted skip of delight all the way back to the car. I am so at peace now as I see my amazing fun buddy beating that bronzed chest hard, ready for the upward climb of defiance, to rekindle all of the extremities that make up necessity of life line. Cut the man and he will bleed Bachata Dance, Hangliding, Double Trapeze, Daily Walking Of Longevity Amongst Natures Landscape and Passion of all things Pangolin.

Yet another ping already for my delight, as I finally figure out which of the many cars in the grounds is my hired vehicle (I can't remember colour or Reg) Derrrrr !!

"What a lovely surprise to see a lovely rare species of white B'fly wearing a pangie emblem today. Thank You xx Indie xx"

I am now ensconced in my hire car in the hospital car park, trying to figure out countless gadgets and triptronics in this ultra mean machine. Mr Tighe your surgeon drives past me in a very large, beautiful, sleek, silver Mercedes convertible. Roof down and not a care in the world.

You know what "He deserves every expensive bit of that flash motor, because today his skill allowed The Princess & The Dragon. ...SEASONS IN TIME OF FUTURE ... JOB WELL DONE

NOW THE ICE MAN COMETH...

This particular species loathes a cold climate, yet can be seen from time to time foraging in snow laden gorse bushes, armed with his trusty camera, seeking out close range encounters with ice formation on greenery and the odd robin or two.

Crunching his way through mammoth layers of snow, Mr I x Snowman is desperately seeking a rare Ice Maiden, whose habitat is in a secret location deep in the tangled woods of Chailey Forest. Before he can even negotiate this tough terrain, he must first undergo the mammoth task of finding a way through "The Ibstock Brickworks" which stand not only as a monument to high quality red brick but a raging furnace of fire. This very dangerous barrier situated by the entrance, he sorely needs to negotiate for continuance of his quest.

On approaching the brickworks this fearless character pulls out his secret weapon. Not for him the standard issue of a H2O fire extinguisher... but a state of the art oxygen gas thrower with full on flame combat features. Ground breaking technology for all "Ice Agents" in the field.

Armed and dangerous he tackles this major obstacle head on or should I say "nozzle on" and finally leaps through the smoldering brick barrier, slipping and a sliding, eventually landing safely on his backside, into the deep cushioned snow of Chailey woods.

Hanging onto various branches and clambering over fallen tree trunks Mr I x Snowman spies a PVC hooded shadowy figure crouching amongst the knarled roots of a massive oak tree. The bright winter sunlight breaking through the trees affords him a glint of reflection from two very sparkly eyes peering at him from under the hood.

"Good Morrow on this crisp cold morn" he politely speaks." Are you in need of a hand out of your woody web?"

"No kind Sir "the hooded one replies "For I am in my habitat of choice. Are you lost in this forest of ice? "she ventures to ask.

He has now ascertained that the hoody one is definitely female and very possibly the ice maiden he is seeking, in disguise. He answers her question.

"I am lost only in this moment of time, as my quest to find the elusive Ice Maiden may have come to fruition. Would you be brave enough to discard your PVC attire and reveal yourself to me, for I am The Intrepid Snowman who has spent a lifetime seeking the Icy, Spicy woman of my dreams."

The creature rose from her mangled roots, unzipped the cladding surrounding her form to reveal this stunning vision of beauty. Golden curls tossed and tumbled around her body as she stepped out of her protective garb. Purple and silver silken lace enrobed her curvaceous stature. Long, sanguine limbs seemed to flail in the cold air as she moved slowly toward him.

He gasped in awe of this Ice Maiden, now wrapped around him like a snake to it's prey. Oh how he had waited for this singular moment of ecstasy. Frenzied desire overtook body and mind, causing every morsel of his being to tremble with anticipation. This Iced temptress orchestrated a fantasy of pure erotica as she writhed over his body in tune with her skilled craft.

Just as Mr I x Snowman reached the heights of complete and utter fulfillment, the heat of the moment had a sting in it's tale... THE ICE MAN MELTED!!!!!! LOST FOREVER IN A PUDDLE. The Ice Maiden had taken yet another victim to add to her repertoire of many a hunter fallen foul of mythical curiosity has many a melting moment...

I hope you like my "Ice Tale" Tatty D x

From your Butterfly Princess with the WARMEST OF SMILES >!<

Xxx Xxx

HE SOARS LIKE AN EAGLE...

High in a clear blue sky, the red winged pilot steers his trusty craft between thermals. Lifting, gliding, dropping on occasion as the wind takes a slight hold but always resolute to maintain the height he needs to stay airborne.

Today is forecast as near perfect conditions for hang gliding pursuits. Mr Red I x runs at a fast pace and conducts the perfect take off to climb skywards. A satisfied smile and a happy heart lift his spirit to great heights.

Watching intently from a nearby cliff top, perched high in the rock face is a beautiful golden eagle. This flamboyant female bird of prey has been looking for a suitable mate for many months. It just so happens that this particular bird has a fondness for the colour red. As a creature whose eyesight is normally high vision for both spotting and hunting food supply, it's a grave travesty that this elegant feathered creature has lost much of her focus due to an old eye injury sustained as a fledgling whilst learning to fly. Red is the one colour still strong enough for her recognition.

So it is not perchance that Goldeneye is following every movement of Mr Red I's x flight. Many days and nights have gone by as the elegant feathered eagle eagerly awaits each visit of the magnificent Red Winged Creature she has fallen in love with. Today she feels brave enough to take off from her hideaway on the cliff edge and attempt to fly in sync with her unrequited obsession.

Mr Red I x feels so at peace up here amongst the azure blue skies, his concentration is paramount yet his thoughts wander to the loneliness of the long distance flyer. How he would love to find that final piece of the jigsaw to make his full on, extreme life complete. A fellow hang glider would be a bonus but female flyers are a minority breed. It's at that moment he spots enormous wings just above and to the right of his machine. "What The F***k "is Red I's x knee jerk response. Panic begins to set in as he fears this golden feathered creature with a massive wing span to match his silken red pairing, will crash down upon him and take them both to catastrophic endings.

Fear turns to admiration as he realizes that the golden one is flying alongside him, in sync, emulating his every movement of flight. "Wow pretty impressive "he shouts across but his words get lost in the wind rushes. "If this bird of prey were a woman, she would be my perfect partner in time" Red I x mutters to himself.

It's time to make a landing, he has been up in the skies for far too long now and the thermals are beginning to fade. Sadness sets in as he realizes the amazing goldeneye will have to be left behind to the elements and the giddy moments of the last hour will be a fading memory. He looks across at his new trusty companion and gives a hand to forehead salute of appreciation. The golden eagle lets out a huge cry of delight, flaps her magnificent wings one last time, then soars off toward the cliff top into the safe haven adopted. She will reside there with anticipation, waiting ever so patiently for the return of her true soulmate, who today finally acknowledged her as a really cool bird with flying skills as adept as his own.

TWO HANG GLIDERS IN UNISON & MASTERS OF THE SKIES... <\> <\>

Xxx Xxx Love Polly

Non Flyer But Great Navigator Of Smiles

TWO WISE OL PALS...

Forget the adage ' One Man & His Dog ' Here stands ' One Maverick & His Trusty Sidekick '

Note the almost ventriloquist like interaction between these two species. Not for them "A Gottle Of Geer "more like "Chuck us a chick quick mate or else "

The feathered one appears to be admiring his friend's headgear, with this profound thought crossing his tiny owl like mind... "Where Did You Get THAT HAT Man "

OR.. He could be thinking... "Drop me in that mega puddle of water and your wellies will end up well shredded "This angry owl can shred up a yellow pages with his mega sharp talons in minutes, producing a confetti like mess that an electric shredder could not even begin to compete with.

Look at the sheer admiration Maverick holds in that momentary gaze toward his feathered friend. Such an endearing smile of remembrance for all of the wondrous times shared as wise man and bird of prey. Many flights of fancy onto a gloved hand, wings outstretched and feathers preened for photogenic purpose. Quiet moments sitting to hand in the late evening sun, a shared bench for quality time Together.

They say a man's best friend is his dog.. Well suffice to say "they got that one wrong "in this instance.. This man' s best friend is the beautiful, charismatic creature he took under his wing and nurtured, many moons ago.

HIS NAME IS LUNA & HE IS A GREAT HORNED OWL

From Your Mutual Admirer.. Of Both Species <3 <3

Xxx Xxx

THIS IS THE LESSER SPOTTED MAN O MAN....

Most likely to be found inhabiting cliff tops in and around the South Downs area. Although he has been known to frequent the pebbled beaches at the foot of the seven sisters on occasion.

You will notice from this picture he is in the throws of his native ritual dance, performed on many a summers day to attract the female of the species woman et woman. His stance is provocative to her mating instinct, plus his natural scent of salty flesh provides just enough enticement to satisfy her peppered palate.

Not for the fainthearted, the eventual coupling of "man o et woman "is a very saucy spectacle indeed. Spicing up each others libido, both parties curry favor upon favor before collapsing in a heap amongst the herbaceous undergrowth to bask in the aftermath of carnivorous capers.

A relative feast of delight is to be savored in the afterglow for body and mind, allowing both a moment of reflection before each departs back to their respective havens on the far side of the sugary white cliffs, lifted tall from the deep blue ocean, basking resplendent in the mid afternoon sunshine.

Yet another day of conquest for man o man and his enigmatic smile. Who knows what tomorrow may bring?? As sure eggs are oval he will clamber up that cliff face once again, adopt his stance of invite and play statues all day long until like choco to holic ... fair maiden melts to his charm.

From your Woman O Woman who adores chocolate and posers..

Xxx Xxx

WELCOME TO MY DOMAIN

The Kingdom Of Poppy Fields where I reign supreme. For I am the self appointed, continuously knighted Majesty of the realm, where the beautiful red, black eyed poppies live in harmony and tranquility.

It is my good fortune to be able to meander my treasured land on a daily basis, complimenting my subjects on their grace and beauty, as they sway in time with the elements of nature. Do not be misled by the delicacy of my charges for they may give the appearance of fragility to the naked eye but within their stamen of darkness lies an explosive element known as opium.

This powerful, mind bending substance is banned by society, yet look back in time and testament to the many medicinal qualities "the dark seeds of the poppy" can tell many a tale of culture and folklore, miracle cures and mayhem. Criminal elements cast a stain on the beauty of poppy yet these precious flowers still stand tall in their own right as one of natures jewels in the crown.

Do not think I rule my Poppy Kingdom alone. It is my great fortune to be able to share my royal office with the "Beautiful Poppy Princess "She who brings a wealth of sunny smiles as a given to our nurtured subjects. For it is the radiant sunshine of her smile that allows everything to grow so magnificently, strength to face the elements and defiance to overcome adversity.

RED ... Is for Redemption of all things possible. Possibilities are endless as the rich red flowers blossom and swathe our fields with the glory of time and a long lasting memorial to times gone by.

From Your Polly Poppied.. Scattering her petals of smiles

Xxx Xxx <3 <3

See before you the modern day version of The Long Man Of Wilmington.. Known as The Longer Man Of Smallfield.

He may not reside on Wendover Hill or be 235 feet tall. Neither is he likely to be etched into the chalk and flint of the South Downs National Park. To not have a local Brewery as his namesake is definitely not a problem for this time traveller.

Why??? You may ask.. Well his own unique blue print has stood the test of time

The Longer Man lives near an Inter National Airport LGW. His footprints of outline are etched into the sands of the Sahara & Namib Deserts for all time. A tribute to his namesake is a hand carved Terra cotta plaque fixed to the wall of a historic building near Timbuktu.

No one knows where The Long Man came from or how he materialized into the hillside. Still one of natures mysteries his outline has been renovated and restored over the years for posterity of attraction.

Many cultures know where The Longer Man comes from. A thirst for knowledge, the world and it's inhabitants were the catalysts for a lifelong exploration of the same. A personal quest taking him through many global continents, meeting peoples of very diverse nationalities and creeds. Leaving behind long lasting friendships and admirers of his natural curiosity.

The Long Man will be tangible for passers by for as long as conservationists choose to continue restoration as time continues erode his image.

As for The Longer Man, erosion of age may be a given but just like his counterpart restoration and longevity lie in the hearts and minds of generations to come who will have access to document of his blueprint.

In Admiration Of Both Long & Especially Longer For He Is Etched In My Heart For A Lifetime <3 Xxx

Giddy Up.. Giddy Up my four legged friend. Where shall we ride out to on this fine day? Along tracks and trails, over the hills and far away

Hold on tight to my reins for dearest life Let's gallop awhile and increase our speed Sit tall and proud on your trusty steed

I know some quaint and quirky places Let's go explore a windmill or two

A haven at Cuckmere to name but a few

Riverside walk meanders in Isfield
Seven sisters with bright chalky white faces
Chailey is quietly common with wide open spaces

Arlington has a reservoir to it's name

Bright colored meadow with butterflies fluttering abound

A spring in our step as we stride round and around

Shingle beach scattering pebbles onto the shoreline Cliff top hill climb many spectacular views to admire Gulls flying overhead so very close to the wire

Ditchling has a beacon that strikes not a light Many times we have trod it's various pathways to follow
Height was a virtue for scenery to soak up and swallow

Another "A" Listed reservoir walk boasting a famous viaduct
Bridges to cross with gentle green hills to climb Sailboats across the water bob with the tide and time

Many footsteps imprinted on our wondrous land-scape
Shared mother nature at it's finest for all seasons
Question ye not the rhyme or the reasons

Tread Softly In My Dreams.. leave gentle hoof prints upon my heart

Your fellow rider through the storm Xxx Xxx

Blah Blah Black Sheep...Weed
Have you any salty slime
Yes Sir.. Yes Sir
Three bags at a time.

One for the master mariner
One for the sultry mermaid
And one for the little shellfish
Who swims along with the tide

Shaun The Sheep.. Weed went out one day
Over the hills and far away
Mother sheep..weed went Blah Blah Blah
And Shaun and his sheep came rolling home.

Shaun The Sheep.. Weed sat on a wall
Shaun The Sheep.. Weed had a great fall
All the sea horses and all the Sea men
Couldn't put Shauny together again.

Little Boy Blue come blow your horn
Shaun The Sheep.. Weed is in the meadow
And The Cows are eating the corn
Spring has finally sprung forth in all it's glory

Boing.. Boing..   Y Boing

                  G

                N

              I

            O

          B

Your Sheepish Dummy Sucking Nursery Rhymer

Xxx Xxx

Scaly Mammal A..

This nocturnal creature can be found amongst densely wooded climes in parts of Africa and Asia. Known for it's secrecy and ability to camouflage itself you would struggle to locate it at the best of times.

Pangolins defensive keratin scales protect them from predators. The main diet of these animals is ants and termites. Their tongues are as long as their bodies which is great for foraging. The claws they carry on their feet are excellent for digging up termites nests or burying themselves into mounds for safety.

On the downside these amazing creatures are the most hunted species on the planet which has now led to the classification of most endangered animals. The scales that are the Pangolin's most endearing feature are gold dust to criminal cartels who make thousands of dollars from the sale of the same ground down for use in Chinese herbal medicines. Bodies sold to foreign food outlets as a delicacy in certain disreputable underground restaurants.

Fortunately world wide awareness of their plight is increasing month on month, thanks to the hard work and publicity generated by dedicated conservationists intent on stopping this despicable situation once and for all. Governments of certain countries are now stepping up their efforts to make an example of the poachers caught, by giving them harsh jail sentences and massive fines. Let us all hope for a brighter future for these cute, harmless creatures of the night.

Scaly Mammal B..

This creature can be found in the depths of the Sussex Countryside. Mostly out and about in daylight, many guises are adopted to avoid recognition. A penguin hat seems to be the favorite disguise, closely followed by an Australian Bush Tracker number complete with bird's feather. A bright blue anorak is sometimes worn to scare off unwanted predators.

This mammal has a very tangoed skin color due to time spent in strong sunlight minus a top. It's light grey, long plumage is it's most endearing feature and trademark look. A hunter, gatherer is indicative to this species. A collection of all things appertaining to mother nature is to be found in it's den.

Mammal B.. Has a penchant for Owls and Butterflies. Infact it is regularly hunted by The Famous Princess Butterfly from The Kingdom of the same. Much sought after for personal pleasuring of the winged fluttery one, no holds are barred in pursuit of ultimate satisfaction.

This unique mammal is also now very endangered. Conservationists near and dear are working hard for survival purpose. Absolutely non replaceable in any way, shape or form, this amazing creature has created a benchmark so high, achievements of pride for eternity and a legacy for many generations of future to learn from.

How much alike are Mammals A & B .. But so very unique in their "own right

"Your AB supporter & winged companion for preservation >!<

They seek him here.. They seek him there

The Elusive Charmer of The Snake Kingdom is nowhere

To be found...

This reptilian, six pack wielding Indie J x is always hiding in precarious places in Jungle climes.

He has a sixth sense for intruder danger, a knack of knowing just when to camouflage himself from the hunters who stand to make mega bucks from his capture.

A bounty was placed on his shoulder length grey mullet many years ago by his greatest rival and adversary.. Jungle Jim. Why the animosity between these two great explorers?? Well !!! Back in the day they set up a snake performing project to entertain the many foreign reprobates who fancied themselves as modern day David Attenboroughs, tramping all over the jungle territory so very precious to these two avid explorers. The gung ho visitors showed little regard for the tropical terrain or the many wonderful creatures housed within. They were just hellbent on bagging a trophy or two to show off to their fellow countrymen back home. So Indie and Jim set up this "Bag A Snake Scam" to tempt these idiots. There was however a very painful sting in the tail.

Indie would hold several snakes, allowing them to wind and slither their scaly bodies all over his torso. Lulling the visitors into a false sense of security he would invite them to do the same and should they be able to entice the snakes into the basket on the ground nearby, they could choose one to take away... No questions asked.

What these unsuspecting duffers did not know was that tucked away in the basket was a very venomous variety of snake who with one agonising bite would render the recipient a gibbering wreck, not fatal but powerful enough to send that person into a mad frenzy. Jungle Jim would then take a polaroid picture of this spectacle and when calm once again prevailed, blackmail would be the order of the day to save embarrassment of cowardice. Money for snake conservation purpose changed hands and sad photo was duly handed over to it's not so brave participant.

This lucrative enterprise was successful for several years and both Intrepids made sure all monies gained were used for the wellbeing of not only the snakes but for all of the other animals living in this territory. Then treachery struck. Indie J discovered that his trusty partner had infact been filtering large amounts of money into a plan to tear down the jungle for redevelopment of a swanky hotel and theme park which would render all of the jungle creatures homeless or even worse wiped out!!! Incensed and bewildered revenge was precision planned.

Gathering together hundreds of his charming snakes, Indie J set them up in as many jungle trees as possible and lay in wait until the surveyors arrived with their ladders and cameras to take stock of the proposed development area. As the team climbed up their various ladders the snakes slithered from their hiding places and struck painful venomous stings into all and sundry. The surveyors fell into a mad frenzy of fear and panic as they were chased up and down their ladders by these slithering creatures.

The upshot of this drama was "A definite no go area for development.. Too flipping dangerous to clear" Jungle Jim was apocalyptic and put out a bounty on Indie J x and to this day each can be found seeking and eluding constant. Jim climbing up his ladder on the lookout and Indie slithering down trees with his trusty snakes.

You could say .. "IT'S BECOME A GREAT GAME OF SNAKES & LADDERS

From your "Dicey" Lady Polly

Xxx Xxx

I am a Hobbit of habitual tree trunk habitat. My home is made out of the finest natural barking wood. Hollowed out to perfection as I set my benchmark to the highest of oaks.

Willow be my native language, lots of vowels and twiglet connotations. Many rings of aging surround my solid trunk to remind me to count up the years.

Leaves are my chosen decoration to adorn the uppermost heights of my haven. Algae is a cladding of insulation and protection for purpose.

Roots run deep snaking a safe and permanent anchor to hold steadfast this abode. Soil of the earth provides fodder for the same.

I sit here quietly and watch the world, outside my hollow haven, go by. The sun bestows its gracious warmth upon my face each morn. As evening falls I am privileged to bathe in the natural glow of a harvest moon.

Spring allows me the beauty of blossom and bees. New beginning of life surrounds me.

Summer comes into view enthralling me with many colours of flora and fauna. Butterflies dance before me to their favorite tune of flutterative harmony.

Autumn brings forth harvest hues of browns and golds. My overhead leafy canopy dissipates but I am safe in the knowledge it will return again the following Spring.

Winter falls of snow to weight my branches, yet so very soft of texture. Icicles become my habitats decoration of frozen kaleidoscope.

A HOBBIT FOR ALL SEASONS ... SAFE HERE IN MY TREE OF LIFE

Your Seasonal Fluttery Favorite >!<

Xxx Xxx

I see the moon and the moon sees me
The sunshine of your smile is my sight to see
Warmth of diverse character upon me bestow
New places of learning wherever we may go

How deep is that valley how high be this hill
Many long roads to travel dreams they fulfill
Castles of splendor so high in the air
Mansions for mayhem too dark with despair

Carve out our names for posterity's sake
This Dragon & his Princess a true scenario they make
Of scenic adventure many places to behold
The storytellers folklore spun in such precious gold

May the moon throw forth his merry beams
The Sun step forward to shine on magnificent schemes
Twinkle with abandon amongst many luminous stars
Let's pack up this crazy life and begin again... ON MARS

From Your Very Own Sunny Moonbeam Earthling
Xxx Xxx

FLORA & FAUNA

Where is the Snapdragon to be found in these parts you ask??

Posing yet again amongst the greenery. Still roaming the countryside fauning over Flora. You would think after all this time he would have given up his relentless pursuit of this colorful maiden and just settled for plain ol Buttercup, or even Daisy may have been an option had he not picked off her petals during their first meeting.

Snapdragon has a bit of a reputation around here as a lover of stamen. Lily told Iris that he couldn't keep his eyes off her tendrils when they went out on a first date. Last one too as it happens, no way was she putting em out there until at least the fifth date. Lily had no intention of following in the footsteps of Rose who well and truly got her prickles into Snapdragon on their first date. Such a thorny, dusky hussy.

Whatever happened to Jasmine who was reportedly the love of Snapdragons life. No one seemed to know where she had fled too and he certainly was not forthcoming as to the fragrant lady's whereabouts these days, although gossip has it she photosynthesized and settled down in blissful harmony with Honeysuckle.

Unbeknown to Snapdragon, there is one other waiting in the wings for his undivided attention. What rare flower of fragrance might this be? Well here comes the twist in the tale.. The wings in waiting belong to non other than the Precious Princess Of The Butterfly Kingdom. WHAT !!! A creature rather than a floral tribute.

Well they do say you should try everything once in this life. Who knows... A brand new species could emerge from this coupling.

"SNAP BUTTER DRAGON FLY "

(a slippery little succor >!<)

From Flora now intertwined with Fauna in pastures green with pleasant landscape.

Xxx Xxx

THESE BOOTS WERE MADE FOR WALKING

These boots are made for walking and that's just what they'll do

One of these days these boots are going to walk all over you

"Ooh Yes Please.. I Adore Footprints "

Although our lives journeys on occasion have kept us apart

I am with you, you are with me always.. In my heart

"We have rambled and preambled many a mile chuck "

Can you walk a mile in my shoes to see how far I've been

To tread the marks I've made along many a path unseen

"Would that be a kilometer or a continent my dearest "

I stumbled on the cobbles of pathways old and new

Waded through the bogs, stuck in mud a fair ol few

"But you always emerge smelling of scented sensibility oh mucky one "

I soldier on, the journey often daunting and treacherous too

With the peak just so close yet too faraway to make do

"Strive amongst the struggle, one step at a time Dear Heart "

Have you ever been in my shoes to walk the golden mile

Catch me when I stumble, with your enigmatic smile

"Tread along with me so I can catch you if you fall over "

Your Partner on the long & winding road.. With her own BOOTS TO BOOT

Xxxxx

An Enigmatic Outfit

CATALOGUE BOY..

Lives between pages of many a popular glossy magazine.
Poses a plenty with not a hair out of place, that would be unseen
Takes trips to the seashore to maintain his healthy, glowing tan
Vanity or self styled preservation here cometh the man

Travels great mileage for shoots all over the land
Definitely not the green variety just professional camera to hand
Wardrobe with style and grace chosen for look of pleasure
Clothing of the highest couture always made to measure

Another suitcase via airport to warm exotic foreign land
First class travel, sleeper seat with smoothest malbec to hand
Chauffeur driven on route to the perfect scenic location
Numerous worldwide countries, what an exacting vocation

Life in the fast lane means constant in front of a lens
Snapped and preened to perfection for pleasure of tens
Of fans in their thousands that flick through the pages where
Stands "Catalogue Boy "flying high on a wing and a prayer

From Your Catalogue Groupie
Who Loves To Flick Through Your Pages
Xxx Xxx

The Shadow Of Your Smile

SHADOW DANCERS...

We lay our shadows down amongst the soft, silken strands of grass
Languish awhile, stretch out weary limbs to soak up respite
Caress strokes of tender flesh, map each nerve ending with intent
Flex finger movement to create frission with wanton outcome

Apart we are mere mortals walking aimlessly in many circles
Together a mutual caste is silhouetted, blended of a defining shape
Symmetry becomes asymmetric, picture perfect and pleasing on the eye
Looks are not visual, yet shapes of admiration visible for viewing

This valley of shadows we walk, feel only the warmth and brightness within
How light are the steps we synchronize in unison for sure footed strength
Tallest of figures we stretch out long and hard to face the rack of life
Harmony and grace be our watchword... Always in step for shadow dancing to perfection

From Your Princess.. Always Shadow Dancing With Her Dragon

Xxx Xxx

PIRATE OR LANDLUBBER XX

At woods edge shadows of the sun nestle
Humid air allows floating ballrooms
Where midges dance brief lives away
Lichen scaled trees where a leaf falls
Emerald mosses myriad mound

Pale toadstools poke up from beneath the ground
The pirate stands under an unseen warblers silk song
Rippling through the echoes amongst branches sturdy

Sun warm on one side casts reflection of bandana patterns
Kaleidoscope smile glints colour bright and beautiful

How green is this grass of many woodland giants
Zigzagging each splendid blade to pointed perfection

Man from bountiful sea stands converted... to Lubber of the land

From Your Woodland Fairy Princess

Xxx Xxx

Many a thing you know you ought to tell us Many a thing we hope to understand

When you were an infant you spoke not in childish tone Put away those plastic toys and go seek your fortune

Alone on the hillside the vision becomes clear to mind

The wealth you carry has no monetary value Gold lies in them there countries yet to explore Their tapestry woven forever in piece of mind

Why idle away the hours when the world is your oyster

The boy took on the mantle of mass exploration Driven by heart nurtured for desire of learning Vast fonts of knowledge quenched a thirst within

Journeys within this lifetime fuelled by curiosity Landscape beyond deserts of shifting sands Deepest dark night skies owned by the universe Planetarium for many stars their secrets forever held

Seek not the answers to a multitude of questions

Just bask in the beautiful cultures of many sights seen The pearl in the oyster was yours for the taking

The boy in the picture was the man who became

KING OF THE WORLD

From your Princess In Waiting

Xxx Xxx

I see the world as the world sees me
High in the sky I'me as happy as can be
Flying like a bird my spirit soars free
Miniature trees of greenery below me I see

How refreshing is the pure air that I breathe
Senses heightened a good flight to achieve
Many thermals of navigation yet to perceive
Staying power is paramount I have no wish to leave

How deep is that gully a river runs through it
Fed by an awesome waterfall I had better not hit
Turns are important secured by wings that fit
Supported by precision metal bars on which they sit

I fly like a great eagle of the golden kind
How lucky am I for this pleasure of mind
It's life for the taking of treasures I find
Hang gliding is a man and his wings a soul to bind

From The Smiley Princess.. Whom you have taken to great heights

Xxx Xxx ;0))))

Spinning Between Constellation To Dreams...
She Dances

Remember when we danced.. For the very first time together

I was so wooden and reticent of how to begin those first few salsa steps

All around me was rhythm, wiggly bottoms (male & female), music to a beat I had not encountered before for dance purpose.

You were so reassuring and confident in your words and outlook for practice equals improved performance. Gently but firmly you led me into those first few salsa steps..forward 123 back 123..

Left hand placed just below your shoulder line but not quite at chest level. Resting gently but with frission. Listen to the beat of the music playing, let your body tune in to the rhythm, trust my hands to guide you in the right direction, SMILE.. You said.

Nervous of all this newness, yet excited for the headiness of salsa dancing.

Apologies for stepping on your feet on occasion, you accepted graciously with your enigmatic smile.

One giant step further.. Into the land of Bachata (Love De Girl) such intoxicating passion of body movements. Sexy, sassy, erotic couplings, limbs synchronized to perfection, every movement honed for visible adoration. A whole new world for the taking, making practice, practice, practice far from perfect, yet perfection for my soul to savor.

We stepped into a darkened room, I stood and watched your solo performance in awe. It was very erotic.

This crazy, sexy man dressed all in black. Bachata movement of intent before me. Fedora worn with such style for temptation.

One jaunty tip of the same and I was hooked.. For eternity

From Your Princess With Her Posh Red Dancing Shoes

Xxx Xxx

A DRAGON TO HAND OF NOTE... ERIETY

His Lairy Stance Is Tall & Proud
Roar Of Breath So Fiery & Loud
Stretching Out To Engulf His Prey
Through Deep Dark Forest He Forges His Way

This Beautiful Maiden With Gossamer Wings
A Delightful Creature To Her Kingdom She Brings
Graceful Qualities Of Mirth & Dance
A True Princess Of Nature Spied At A Glance

By The Fearsome Dragon Strong Of Intent
Watching & Waiting With Flame To Vent
For Princess Butterfly He Longs To Consume
A Lust Of Being To Fulfill Desire Of Doom

He Sees Her Dancing Bathed In The Light Of Moon
Beams Of Sparkling Silver She Sways In Tune
Gossamer Wings Create Diamonds Precious Of Reflection
Entranced.. The Dragon Sees Before Him Ultimate Perfection

This Specimen Of Beauty He Has Need To Own
Furnace Of Fire Allows Loud Carnal Moan
Consume All Want Of Natures Beast
Upon Her Lithe Sensual Body He Longs To Feast

Entwined In Tendrils Of Wanton Desire
Princess Butterfly Succumbs To The Fire
Lost In The Flames Of Heightened Pleasure
She Dances With Her Dragon.. Now His Forever
From Your "Revolutionary "Richmond Princess

SHERPA RANKIN HAS GONE WALKABOUT

The Intrepid Traveller Sherpa Rankin....

Has been following the trail of stoned monuments throughout the length and breadth of The Southdowns Way.

Never one to turn down the calling of natures finest brickworks, he begins the arduous task of seeking out various rock formations ranging from grit to granite, logging every porous detail on his slate pad using only the finest of pure white chalk.

The journey throws up some boulder size moments of joy to cement his belief that all that glitters in this terrain is definitely top grade sandstone. Boots coated in molten clay, Sherpa Rankin strides enthusiastically along the numerous pathways and trails with monumental enthusiasm to complete the given task. His foot- hold firm of stomping ground.

Has he lost his marbled mind taking up this challenge? The routes are not simple of stoney ground, more like tortuous jagged slag heaps. Coalface climbs are inevitable interspersed with craggy vales. Shingle pours it's sharp, gritty edges into every boot orifice. Definitely not for the faint hearted more for the solid rocker with a heart of ironstone.

Fear ye not.. Determination and resilience be his guide. One man, two boots, a flak jacket, penguin hat, cool shades and a very strong will to survive has allowed Sherpa Rankin to add many solid stone monuments to his repertoire and guess what ?? He is still out there treading the path and counting yet more conquered milestones in the distance ahead.

True Sherpa integrity with Intrepid resilience.. Maketh The Man

From The Princess Who Is Proud To Walk Always By Your Side >!<

Xxx Xxx

I SHAKE HANDS WITH MY NEMESIS

Time & Tide Wait For No One ...

We tread this earth with its timeless mansions of labyrinth
Make our mark with many a tale to tell... the fruits of our loins bear witness
What a grand entrance in the scheme of things so lucky to be born
Life is a gift to savor.... Reckless in youth yet so much appreciated for senior years

Collectable treasures of memories stored away.. They mark our very existence
Countless sunshine days and moonlit nights scattered with a zillion stars
Weave their way through our very own planetarium of awesome sight
Wonders too complex to measure yet ours for the taking and making of dreams

How high is that mountain.. too low be the valley before us
Yet we survive the many slings and arrows of discontent
Allowing ourselves the joyful time of living amongst this complex
Tapestry of life.. It's wonders to perform

The time comes for us all when the tide goes out and never returns
Strength of defiance we cling on to this driftwood of longevity
Bold as brass the final corner is fought.... For as long as it takes
Tick Tock goes the giant clock.. It's time to meet and greet our nemesis.

For the countless sunshine days.. And awesome moonlit nights we have treasured together
Your very own "Fairytale Princess Polly "

Xxx Xxx

42

THE PIRATE & POLLYANNA

THE PIRATE & POLLYANNA

What does Pollyanna mean?

She is a person characterized by irrepressible optimism and has a tendency to find good in everything. Sweet tempered and good natured even in adversity.

Let the adventure begin...

He is awaiting the arrival of his trusty companion for this journey of swashbuckling potential. Trunk packed full of booty and doubloons, the route is mapped, compass at the ready. The Pirate and Pollyanna set out to far off lands and distant shores.

The journey is long and tiring, darkness ensues as they land at point of destination.

Maps prove fruitless as a wrong turning is taken allowing many twists and turns, lost in the wilderness, until by sheer determination of my Pirate and a bit of good direction from a local inhabitant, we have finally reached The Rolling Stone Overnighter in Boco Chico. Basic accommodation with non working shower facilities, two very weary travelers hit the sack for respite. Loud music and revelry can be heard until the early hours. The local youngsters are partying hard. Drugs, prevalent, had already been offered to The Pirate on arrival at this seedy place. He had swerved the subject eloquently in broken Spanish dialogue, avoiding confrontation with the dodgy, high on a substance dealer, hassling for gold coins. Finally peace and quiet reigned around 3am and blessed sleep overcame downcast beginnings.

Breakfast is a hungry need, as food on the journey here was in short supply. Ahoy there, another Pirate is spotted at the food bench, complete with grey matted hair, red bandanna and missing a right arm. Good banter ensues as this meeting of fellow adventurer was not expected. The surroundings are rustic colonial, cluttered, ramshackle yet littered with color of deep pink blossom and rich green palm trees standing tall and strong, their spiky branches flowing gently in the breeze. The morning sky is the deepest of blue and the warmth of the hot sun feels like glowing ember to my pale European skin. For me, Pollyanna, this is a journey into the unknown with a Pirate who has pillaged my world for several years, but never until now has dared to take the risk of exploration with a fledgling who wishes to share some of the adventure of his way of life. I have set out on my journey with an open mind and safe kharma, wishing to push a few boundaries in the company of my trusty Pirate companion.

It is time to move on now to our base for the next seven nights. Good basic food cooked and consumed with relish, fuels us for the next part of the journey. "Heave Ho Me Hearties. "

A new day beckons for The Pirate and Pollyanna to head off up country to seek out refuge for the next seven days. A rustic, thatched white painted casa, our base for exploration of Las Terrenas and Samana Province. Maps in hand, literally, we now need to depart from this drug fueled place, before the shady character encountered the previous evening turns up at the Rolling Stone with his illegal contraband, wishing to relieve us of gold coins.

The morning sun is scorching against a backdrop of deep blue sky, as I savor it's hot rays on my skin. Humidity claws at my throat, as I switch on a fresh air contraption within our mode of transport, for respite. My trusty Pirate and Pollyanna are on the trail at last and arrive safely onto the well made up road for a leisurely two hour journey. Beautiful scenery, so lush green in it's finery of majestic landscape, surrounds us on all sides. Many mango groves and palm trees in abundance vie for prominence. Truly spectacular viewing to feast our eyes upon. The downside to this scenic route is the blaggards we will encounter on the way at four separate barricades. They will demand gold doubloons of varying value before they will open the barriers for continuance of travel. My Pirate companion is contemptuous of the price to pay but has promised to hand over the booty with no swordplay on this occasion.

At last, lighter of coin pouch and hungry for sustenance, we find ourselves on the last leg of the journey. Deep cut gorges into the mountainside throw up giant walls of redstone jagged rock, interspersed with rugged vegetation of countless bushes and trees. Weaving a navigation around many sharp bends we suddenly encounter this stunning view ahead of tropical turquoise bay. Rolling whitewashed surf dances between the deep waves as they wash upon the curved golden sandy beach, glistening with reflection of bright afternoon sunlight. Palm trees edged along the beach, line up tall and erect like cavalry waiting to go into battle. My senses are filled with the breathtaking beauty of this scene that lies before me. Now we need to stop and drink in this sight of color. Hey Ho we spy a monstrous cave cut deep into the mountainside, adjacent to the bay. Black holes are tempting for my Pirate, yet very scary for myself. He is off and striding to explore it's caverns. I follow behind, stumbling of step and wary of what we may encounter inside. Many giant stalagmites and stalactites lay claim to their inheritance of pink and green marbled hues, reflected of color from the natural daylight draping their location. Calm washes over me as the steeped history and beauty of these surroundings simply take my breath away. Amazing.

Now back out into the bright afternoon sun, we race across the highway to the viewing point where recordings are made of the turquoise majestic bay in all it's glory of coastal landscape to behold. "It's time to move on land lubbers "

La Casa Base Camp glints reflective shards of light, bouncing off the white painted walls that gleam in the morning sunshine. A hearty pirate breakfast fuels us both for the mountainous trek of endurance we are about to embark on.

A watery grave is the threat before us if we put one foot or hoof wrong on this trail. Yes the Pirate & Pollyanna are trekking on horseback to the El Limon Waterfall, where a rich bounty of treasure is reputed to be buried amongst the cavernous rocks that lie beneath the mouth of the falls.

We have enlisted the help of two very well paid local guides to lead the way to this buried treasure. However, they are very unaware of the purpose of our journey. They just think we are interested tourists out to see the sights of Dominica and enjoy the scenery. "Ooh Arrrr we hopes they are easily duped "

Halfway along the route, I am struggling with the deep gullies and slippery rocks. Not being on horseback for many a year renders me timid of the beast beneath my buttocks. My trusty Pirate shouts back reassurance but to no avail. My decisive "Get me off this sodding horse "rings out loud and clear thus prompting the two guides to come a running to my rescue. The rest of the journey I will walk on foot, if the locals can do it so can Pollyanna... in determined mode.

At last base camp is in sight, a sojourn in the wilderness to rest and drink the local rum. What be this here in front of us? A table full of silver booty laid out ready for rich pickings. Shall we rob them of their local treasures now, or hold fire until we see if the real reward lies beyond the two hundred steps we must now descend to our final destination of El Limon. A quick wink and a nod from my Pirate companion, whilst purchasing a few blue stone necklaces, let's them off "The Hook" (scuse the pun)

The plan on arrival at the falls is for me to distract our guides, whilst himself scours the rocky crevices for gold dubloons. "Easy peesy, El Limon squeezy" as I strip down to my bathing costume and shimmy through the rippling foam that cascades all around me from the breathtaking wall of water crashing down the rock face from a dizzy height. The guys sit by the rock pool, mesmerized, as my trusty Pirate companion plunders the near-bye caverns, gathering as much gold as he can carry in the secret pockets of his brass buttoned coat and baggy breeches.

It's a very long, weary trek back to our start point but one of great triumph, for not only did our plan run smoothly with no need of taking any prisoners, but it also rendered true endurance of a personal nature conquered for posterity.

Morning has broken in our Dominican hideaway. A very late night has taken it's toll on our weary bones. My pirate cap'n had treated me to Lobster on the beach. Not literally.. A beachfront hostelry decked out with hundreds of twinkly lights strung along it's rustic thatched roof had provided us with great repast, complimented with the cathartic sound of rolling waves lapping gently onto the sandy shore. Aye Aye Me Cap'n was as happy as a parrot on his shoulder in a familiar place... Just like home. Serenaded by the local Amigo's allowed my pirate a wry smile. Not quite the raucous drink fueled sea shanties he would normally be heading up.

Fueled by grog and romantic settings, my heave ho hearty Pirate Capn decided a bit of a knees up was fanciable. Not for us the hornblower jig... for this Seadog has hidden talents. A mean Bachata is his speciality dance and just across the street was La Bodega, a stomping ground for the local Bachatero's to hone their craft and show off their sexy moves.

We danced till dawn My Cap'n & I, twirling and swirling, writhing and wiggling. The locals were astonished to see such expertise of movement from "A Gringo"

The music was intoxicating and the rum embued our sensual awareness of both the rhythm of the dance and each other. Magic moments to share forever.

It is decided a quiet, relaxing day of exploration is in order. The Cap'n has pored over his treasure map at length and decided we could find our pot of gold at Las Galeras a coastal haven of golden sand and turquoise seas.

Driving there is a bumpy affair of road bearing potholes and evil protruding ramps in situ through the various townships on route. Fortunately our motor is equipped to just about cope with all, although a few major swerves here and there are very necessary at times.

Finally... we are parking up at our destination and starving hungry. Having passed several eateries coming into Las Galeras we did wonder if there would be anywhere on the actual beach to eat. Fear ye not a wooden ramshackle beach shack is tucked away in a corner of the sandy beach between rusting old boats and a cluster of very tall palm trees.

Worn out trestle tables and gnarled benches provide the furnishings, whilst a pungent smell of Cajun spices delight the nostrils. We are not disappointed with our fayre, it is absolutely delicious. The cap'n orders home made chicken soup & rice and I sample the locally caught Dominican fried squid with baked rustic bread. Washed down with home made maracuya juice (passion fruit) The Cap'n says "Don't be misled by appearance.. The scruffiest is sometimes a treasure trove of delights" I will give him that one as it is a truly local, scrumptious lunch in the unlike- liest of surroundings.

We watch a few of the local men playing dominican draughts for awhile. They get very passionate for the winning of the same, slamming their black and white round counters on to the game board with gusto. Much banter and laughter make it a very jolly affair. This is a much played pastime throughout the Dominican Republic. A national treasure... The Cap'n and I though, not to be swayed, are looking for a much bigger prize.. Buried Treasure Me Hearties !!!!!

The hot white sand and rolling surf beckons and we wander off in search of our end goal. We scour the beach, barefoot, paddle in the gentle surf searching amongst the many rock pools. We walk the length of the whole bay, sadly no treasure here, just a few fallen trees, slow moving crabs and piles of dried out mangled barnacles.

Languishing on the soft, warm sand of Playa Galeras in the afternoon sunshine, looking out to far horizons, against a backdrop of deep turquoise color that is the Atlantic Ocean. Tall, ageless palm trees sway elegantly in the gentle breeze. Calm and serenity wash over us like a soft tidal wave. Paradise lost and found in natures simple tapestry of beauty. Time & Tide stand very still, at this moment, for The Pirate & Pollyanna.

The misty dawn breaks over our Casa Haven.. A very early start for us treasure hunters. 7am post hearty breakfast for fuel, we clamber half asleep into our motor wagon to head off to Samana Bay under the pretext of whale watching. A beautiful winding stretch of not so pot holed road goes before us. Majestic scenery, lush with a hundred different shades of greenery, complimented by many assorted bright colors of flowering beauties, interspersed between the native palm trees swaying so regally in the gentle morning breeze.

Hey Ho I see many ships Cap'n.. Or would that be more like boats... bobbing by the jetty, awaiting many passengers and watchers to laden them decks with the hustle and bustle of curiosity a plenty. My trusty companion has picked the biggest and the best "The Pura Mia "as only a very discerning Pirate would. Heave Ho me hearties tis time to set sail for open water and the spectacle that is known in these parts as "Whale Watching "Each year at around this time thousands of whales migrate to this Provence from far off oceans. It is a time to give new life to the species, allowing the very young to bask in the warm dominican waters, nestling safely beside the underbellies of their birth mothers whilst she teaches them the craft of survival.

12 o clock, 3 o,clock , 1 o,clock.. Quite far off sightings, possibly 6 or 7 whales...many blow spouts but few breeches today.

Our highlight is several minutes alongside a mother and 4 week old calf basking in the midday sun. The cap'n takes many pictures for memory and posterity. Our trip is not in vain, still no clues as to buried treasure, yet treasure trove a plenty watching the beauteous elegance of these gigantic clever creatures as they go about the daily business of subterranean existence.

A quirky local cafe is found tucked down a side street in the port. Home cooked Tortilla served with salad, washed down with a delicious Italian white wine, is just the treat for two hungry explorers... mesmerized of a new experience but still on the lookout for that all important buried treasure.

Slept like a log... After the disaster that was day 6. We had picked a place called Nagua from the local map which indicated old castles and caves. Great place we surmised for buried treasure. After the most horrendous pot holed journey through barren and depressing scenery, the elusive castle and caves were not found, despite further map forays and off road searches. Really frustrating and the waste of a precious day. Despondent and weary the Cap'n & I had returned in not the best of moods, although we did manage to capture some gorgeous sunset/palm photos from a high point on the road into Las Terranas. A sombre meal and an early night seemed the best option all round.

Woke up early on Day 7 with a positive mindset for the day ahead. Finally got my "Beach Day"

As the Cap'n had promised. No hunt today for elusive treasure, just golden sand, turquoise seas and total relaxation. We did hoard a few local treasures though as we shopped, in the town, for a few trinkets and souvenirs to take back home with us for the rest of the crew.

The day was hot and divine in the glorious warmth of sunshine interspersed with amazing scenery to tantalize the senses. We set up camp a few yards from a great beach bar, where we enjoyed a delicious lunch with views to die for. Colorful wooden fishing boats lined up along the golden sand between palm trees as old as yore. Gentle rolling surf whitewashed it's way in toward us, leaving behind in it's wake a deep blue sky bathed in tropical sunshine. The odd flotilla of yachts would occasionally pass our eye line sailing across the horizon on their way to somewhere. We were in a heavenly place at this moment in time.

For the first time ever.. Pollyanna swam in the sea, egged on by my enthusiastic playmate. It was such an achievement. After 20 years of settling for the safety of swimming pools, not only had I swam under a waterfall at El Limon but now "The Sea" could be added to my repertoire.

"Hurrah" shouted my trusty companion from the shoreline where he stood and watched with pride.

The Pirate spent his afternoon sketching or meandering off along the beach to look for possibilities, whilst I languished in the hot sun. We noticed a set of metal hanging bars a few yards away, obviously designed for muscular exercise. Now ....my fellow treasure hunter, apart from Piracy, has another arrow to his bow or should I say peg to his leg. Airiel Hanging. Too good an opportunity to pass by.. Temptation to display one's talents saw the Cap'n perform a few moves on this metal contraption, watched with admiration from a third party, a young eastern European guy, who then preceded to show us his bar skills as well. After a three way jolly discussion of mutual interests, I decided it was my turn to have a go as The Cap'n's hanging partner. A little bit of pretense though as having eaten too many delicacies there was no way he would be able to take my weight...but a bit of trick photography from the Capn's admirer and we made the final result look kosher.

A great day for the pirate and Pollyanna.. Treasure hunting put to one side for a while. An evening meal was truly enjoyed at one of the beach bars at Las Terranas, our respective skins glowing and bronzed from our time spent in the hot sun. We slipped over the road to La Bodega for a few hours of "Cool Bachata "and a drop of rum. We watched the youngsters perform their moves but as ever my Partner In All Things put his unique slant on this sexy dance to the admiration of the locals.. A Gringo excelling at their dance of heritage.

This being our last ditch attempt to seek out the elusive buried treasure, one final destination is sought on our map of discovery. One final journey will take us way down the mountain, followed by a short boat ride from the coastal town of Sanchez to "Los Haitises "A national treasure in this Dominican land. Watery trails, mangrove swamps, ancient caves and exotic birds await our presence, their wonders to unfold.

So it is with great anticipation that the Cap'n & I board the minibus outside our "casa" joining a complete set of strangers, French & Italians, along with our very smiley, charismatic tour guide Henry, meet and greet.

Our journey across to the islands, in a tiny fibre glass boat complete with outboard motor and Dominican sailor to steer, was perfect. Calm turquoise water lapped gently alongside of our little domain, allowing a very relaxed exchange of broken English and hand gestures as we all, on board, got to know a smidgen of each another for a brief moment in time. Warm sunshine bathed this small band of buccaneers, as all nationalities eagerly relished the many magnificent sights and sounds around and about us throughout this amazing, cultural experience.

The Cap'n and I took every opportunity to sneak into dark cavernous corners seeking our end goal... treasure. Apart from a mis placed tarantula spider and many ancient Indian tribal etchings on cave walls, no clues whatsoever threw themselves before us.. We were becoming rather desperate as time was running to a stand still.

Lunch gave us a welcome break, served in a colonial style setting, surrounded by many colorful rocky enclaves, waterfalls cascading into lagoons for bathing and steep climbs leading to scenic viewing, should one have the time and energy after such a mean feast. We two certainly didn't. A ride on a rickety swing was our muster. Me pulling, himself pushing.

With no "Booty" to stash onboard we raggle taggled our way back to land in our trusty motorboat but a very choppy ride, complete with stalled motor due to driftwood jamming the rudder, gave all passengers much cause for concern. The boat man and Henry did a sterling job of keeping spirits buoyant until eventually this little motley crew landed safe and soaking wet back onto dry land, in the welcome port of Sanchez. It was with gratitude that we passed the trusty sailor's soggy cap around, to be filled with doubloons for saving grace.

Our final eventide in Dominican Climes finds The Pirate & Pollyanna wrapped in the atmosphere of our favorite eatery on the beach. "Post Restaurant" This twinkly lit haven, with moonlit ocean views was discovered on day 2 when we walked the length of Las Terranas looking for somewhere posh with morsels to tempt the senses. Tonight in situ is a very lively band of Spanish guitarists .. We christen them "The 3 Amigos "aptly named as there are 3 of them.

The Pirate has swaggered over to have a quiet word and here's me thinking he had decided to join them to show off yet another talent of repertoire. My oh my what element of surprise he orchestrates. What magic web is woven around my very being, a memory to archive, as I am serenaded in true Dominican style by these 3 handsomely rewarded Amigos... "Bachata Romantica "breathes out it's melody of romance into the midnight sky.

A Relaxed last breakfast at our lovely "Casa DR" what a joyful stay with mine hosts Sergio and Kristina..nothing was too much trouble for either and Kristina's quirky Italian cake served with breakfasts was a first for me. Delicious though it was in content and variety, abandonment of this treat was politely conveyed on day 3.

All our booty packed and padlocked, with a change of travel clothing for later, we waved our final goodbye and headed for the beach of Las Terrannas , to camp for the day by our favorite beach bar with a view to "one last ditch attempt "to find our elusive buried treasure. Too many times our end goal had been subject to many distractions in this beautiful, exotic land. It was now or never for discovery of wealth or return home in poverty of failure.

Last minute goodies were purchased with the last of our gold plated doubloons. Included was keepsakes for each of us to decorate the Capn's cabin back in blighty and Pollyanna's bolt hole near the south coast, well sort of... a bit further north inland, give or take 12 miles. Geography and map reading was never my strong point as my Pirate mate would definitely agree with, having been led a merry diverted dance on many walks I had navigated back in Englamd.

This final day was luxurious in a wealth of sunshine and vibrant colours so pleasing on the eye. The Cap'n sketched awhile, perched on his lounger, whilst I paddled along the shoreline kicking up the odd bit of shingle, allowing my bronzed feet warmth of comfort from the gentle whitewashed surf. Lunch is divine, a plateful of healthy ingredients with the added treat of a drop of Dominican rum with our coffee for afters. An afternoon stroll along the soft golden sand allows us this last few hours of precious time to cast our eyes in earnest, seeking out any obvious clues for the "T" WORD...

Time is no longer on our side. So it is with forlorn demeanor we pack up our bits and pieces, change into traveling garb and head back down the costly peage to airborne departure from this place of adventure. The tangible treasure trove was not discovered... It remains here in a rightful place. The "Real Treasure" the Cap'n & I take back with us are the many sights, sounds, colors, expeditions and all of the wonderful experiences savored, to be stored in our memory box for all time....

The Story That Is... The Adventure Of The Pirate & Pollyanna Comes To An End.

This picture saw the very beginning of The Pirate & Pollyanna searching for buried treasure. As the story unfolded it became quite apparent that nothing of tangible value was ever going to be discovered.

A treasure trove of new and exciting experiences, priceless beyond measure, are the true bounty.... spread over the 9 days we spent in The Dominican Republic. All recounted for memory to savor in our lifetime.

The T Shirt Pollyanna wears is a true statement of our "TREASURED "magical moments in this Far Off Land....

HAPPINESS IS... Times With A Pirate In Far Off Lands Trekking to Limony waterfalls and falling off horses. Swimming in cascades of sprayed waterfall frothiness Bluestone silver necklace a bountiful gift Chasing whales around Samana Bay.. Sightings at lots of "O Clocks" Deserted Beaches & Turquoise seas... Je Taime Senor Pablo inscribed in the sand Romantic Beach Restaurants...Gifted Serenade "Romantica Bachata" from my Funny Valentine Historical caves adorned with ancient etchings of centuries gone by carved into stone Mangrove swamps, littered with twisted trunks and life of birds exotica Choppy boat rides and a sodden plucky navigator Acrobatic antics on "beach bars".. Definitely non alcoholic just intoxicating La Bodega dancing in the dark.. The bachata light, of musicality, switched on for Senor Pablo Wizzy, wuzzy "Wasps" around & about the speed bumpy, pothole roads The soothing sounds of the sea & gentle waves lapping around bare feet Swimming in the salty waters of Las Terranes on a hot, sunny "Beach Day" La Casa De Sergio y Cristina brought us the gift of a Dominican place to remember, with many happy moments to enjoy. HAPPINESS STILL IS... Pollyanna & Her Pirate... Imprinted For All Time

WE LIVED <3   WE LAUGHED <3   WE LOVED <3

Dominican Republic
Las Terranas
February 2016

Many moons and countless tears
Can never make up for the lost years
I will now not spend in your passionate embrace
The world you gave me I can never replace

A wonderment of life lived so true
So many loving moments shared with you
I will keep all those memories close to heart
For then we will seldom seem apart

Cherished adventures in the passing of time
A legacy of knowing we shared together
Intimate nights to allow belonging forever
I will wrap up safe in my heart to treasure

I danced with you always in this beautiful life
My world was such a better place to be
With you <3 Dear Heart <3 by my side
May you rest awhile now Indie Dragon

So Peacefully In My Dreams....
Your Butterfly Princess Of Smiles >!<